Wolfgang Amadeus Mozart

COMPLETE STRING QUINTETS

with the Horn and Clarinet Quintets

Wolfgang Amadeus Mozart

COMPLETE STRING QUINTETS

with the Horn and Clarinet Quintets

From the Breitkopf & Härtel
Complete Works Edition

Dover Publications, Inc.
New York

Published in Canada by General Publishing Company, Ltd., 30 Lesmill Road, Don Mills, Toronto, Ontario.
Published in the United Kingdom by Constable and Company, Ltd., 10 Orange Street, London WC2H 7EG.

This Dover edition, first published in 1978, is a republication of *Serie 13 (Quintette für Streichinstrumente)* of *Wolfgang Amadeus Mozart's Werke. Kritisch durchgesehene Gesammtausgabe*, originally published by Breitkopf & Härtel, Leipzig, in 1883. Only "Eine kleine Nachtmusik," not a true quintet, has been omitted.

International Standard Book Number: 0-486-23603-X
Library of Congress Catalog Card Number: 77-88737

Manufactured in the United States of America
Dover Publications, Inc.
180 Varick Street
New York, N.Y. 10014

Contents

	page
String Quintet in B-flat Major, K.174 (1773)	1
String Quintet in C Minor, K.406 (arrangement, 1787, of the Serenade for Wind Instruments, K.388, of 1782)	23
Quintet for Violin, 2 Violas, Violoncello and Horn or 2nd Violoncello in E-flat Major, K.407 (1782)	41
String Quintet in C Major, K.515 (1787)	54
String Quintet in G Minor, K.516 (1787)	86
Quintet for Clarinet, 2 Violins, Viola and Violoncello in A Major, K.581 (1789)	112
String Quintet in D Major, K.593 (1790)	133
String Quintet in E-flat Major, K.614 (1791)	157

Note: The W.A.M. numbers that appear at the foot of the pages of music are the same as the Köchel numbers for the respective compositions.

Wolfgang Amadeus Mozart

COMPLETE STRING QUINTETS

with the Horn and Clarinet Quintets

String Quintet in B-flat Major, K.174

tr
(tr)
fp
f
p

tr
tr
p
p
p
p
p
f
f
f
f
f
f
3
(p)
(p)
(p)
fp
fp
fp
fp
(f)
(f)
(f)
(f)
(f)

p
f
tr
(f)

Adagio.
pp con sordino
pp con sordino
pp con sordino
pp con sordino
pp (con sordino)
f
f
f
f
tr
f
(p)
(p)
(p)
(p)
(p)

fp
pp
f
p
cresc.
tr
(p)

Coda.

Menuetto ma allegretto.

Trio.
Menuetto D. C.

Allegro.

p
p
f
f
f
(f)
(f)
(f)
(f)

tr
tr
tr
tr
tr
tr
tr
tr
tr
3

(f)
(p)
p
f

Coda.

Anhang.*

Dieses Trio ist von Mozart verworfen und das vorn abgedruckte von ihm statt dessen componirt worden. Als selbstständige Composition wird es gleichwohl hier mitgetheilt.

* Supplement: This trio was rejected by Mozart and the one printed above composed in its place. It is presented here nevertheless as an independent composition.

String Quintet in C Minor, K.406

f
sf
fp
p

p
f
sf

p
sf
f
tr

f
sf
p

f
p
sf

Andante.

f
p
cresc.
sfp

p
sfp
sfp
sfp
sfp
sfp
sfp
cresc.
f
f
f
f
f
p
p
p
p
p

Minuetto in Canone.
pp
f
p
sfp
tr

Trio al rovescio.
p
M. D. C. al
Allegro.

f
f
f
f
f
p
p
p
p
p
1ma volta
2da volta

p
f
tr
3

tr
p
fp
sf p

mfp
mfp
mfp
mfp
mfp
mfp
mf
mf
mf
mf
mf
p
p
p

f
f
f
f
pp
mfp
pp
tr

mfp
mfp
mfp
mfp
f
Maggiore.
f
f
f
f
f
tr
tr
p
p
p
p
f
f
f
f
f
tr
tr
tr

Horn Quintet in E-flat Major, K.407

tr
fp
(f)
f
p
pizz.
arco

tr
tr

tr

pizz.
arco
tr

Andante.
tr
3
tr

tr
tr
tr
p
p
p
p
f
f
f
f
p
p
p
p
f
f
f

p
f
3
tr

Allegro.
p
f
tr

tr
p
f
fp

f
tr

String Quintet in C Major, K.515

f
p
f
p
cresc.
cresc.
cresc.
cresc.
f
f
f
f
f
p
p
p
p

f
p
cresc.
f
fp
piano

mfp
mfp
cresc.
f
p
f
cresc.
f
p
f
p
cresc.
f
p
f
p
cresc.
f
f
p
cresc.
f
p
f
p
p
cresc.
cresc.
cresc.
cresc.
cresc.

dolce
(cresc.
(cresc.
(cresc.
(cresc.

p
p
p
p
p
tr
tr
tr
tr
tr
tr
f
p

f
p
f
p
cresc.
cresc.
cresc.
cresc.
cresc.
f
f
f
f
f
p
p
p
p

f
p

tr
f
p
mfp

mfp
cresc.
f
p
1

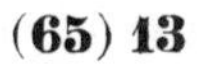

cresc.
tr
f
p
pp

MENUETTO.

Allegretto.

cresc.
f
p
cresc.
f
p
f
W. A. M. 515.

M. D. C.
Andante.

f
p

tr
f
p
sf

dolce

tr
f
p
cresc.
mfp
W. A. M. 515.

pp
pp
pp
pp
pizz.
(Allegro.)
p
p
p
p
p

(mf)
(mf)
(mf)
(mf)
(mf)
(p)
(p)
(p)
(p)
f
f
f
f
f

tr
p
tr

f
f
f
f
f
p
p

f p
p
f
1

(cresc.)

(mf)
(p)
f
p

f
f
f
f
f
tr
tr
tr

tr
p
p
p
p
p
tr
tr
3
3
3
3
3
3

cresc.
f
cresc.
f
cresc.
f
cresc.
f
cresc.
f

String Quintet in G Minor, K.516

f
p
mfp
mf

(cresc.
(cresc.
(cresc.
(cresc.
(cresc.
f)
f
tr
sfp
sf
p
f
W. A. M. 516.

mf
tr
p)
cresc.
mfp
mf
p

mfp
mf
f
p
tr

mfp
mf
p
(cresc.
f)
tr

sfp
p
f
sf
mf
tr
p)

(cresc.)
(cresc.)
(cresc.)
(cresc.)
cresc.)
MINUETTO.
Allegretto.

cresc.
1.
2.
Trio.

tr
tr
1.
2.
Men. da capo.

Adagio ma non troppo.
p con sordino
cresc.
f
p
sfp

cresc.
f
p
mfp
cresc..
pp
sf

cresc.
f
p
sfp
sf
fp
mfp

mfp
mfp
mfp
mfp
mfp
pp
pp
pp
pp
pp
f
p
f
p
p
f
f
f
f
p
p
p
p
pp
pp
pp
pp
pp

Adagio.
senza sordino
p senza sordino
p senza sordino
p senza sordino
pizz.
p senza sordino
arco
pizz.
cresc.
W. A. M. 516.

p
p
p
p
arco
attacca
Allegro.
p
sfp
sfp
fp
fp
fp
fp
fp
fp
f
f
f
f
f
f
f
calando
pp
p
sfp
p
fp
fp
p
p
p
f
p

f
p
1.
2.
tr
cresc.

f
p
fp
cresc.
mf

cresc.
calando

pp
p
sfp
cresc.
f
(mf
mf
p)
1.

2.
tr
f
p
cresc.

p
p
p
p
p
f
f
f
f
p
p
p
p
f
p
f
f
f
f
f
p

p
cresc.
mf
f

f
p
tr.
fp
cresc.

Clarinet Quintet in A Major, K.581

p
p
p
fp
fp
fp
fp
fp
fp
f
f
f
f
p
p
p
pizz.
p

p dolce
pp
pp
pp
pp
sf
cresc.
cresc.
cresc.
arco
cresc.
f
f
f
f
f
f
f
f
f
tr
tr
tr
p dolce
p
p
p

tr
p
f

fp
f
p
pizz.
p dolce
pp

arco
cresc.
cresc.

tr
f
p
cresc.

Larghetto.

p
p *con sordino*
p *con sordino*
p
p

dolce

trmm
f
f
f
f
f
dolce
p
p
p
p

dolce

MENUETTO.
f senza sordino
f senza sordino

Trio I.

M. D. C. senza replica
Trio II.
(p)
pizz.
arco
fp

M. D. C. senza replica
Allegretto con Variationi.

Var. I.
Var. II.
tr
p
f
fp

Var. III.
Var. IV.

fp
fp
f
Adagio.
p
fp
p
p

Allegro.
p
tr
f

String Quintet in D Major, K.593

tr
p
f
sf

p
cresc.
f
tr

tr
p
f

p
sf
f
p
p
p
p

Larghetto.
p dol.
p
p
p
f p
rf p
rf p
rf p
rf p
rf p
Tempo I.
tr
p
p
p
p
p
f
f
f
f
f

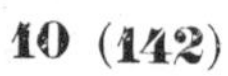

Adagio.
p
f
fp
cresc.
tr
6
3

f
p
fp
tr
(p)
(♯)
cresc.

f
f
f
f
f
p
p
p
p
cresc.
cresc.
cresc.
cresc.
cresc.
pizz.
arco
(p
cresc.)
p
(p)

tr
f
p
fp
(p)

f
p
tr
6
pp

MENUETTO.
Allegretto.

Trio.
p
pizz.
arco
f
Menuetto da capo

FINALE.
Allegro.
p
cresc.
f
1

2.
tr
f
p

p

f
p
f
p
f

cresc.
p
f
tr

tr
tr
p
p
p
p
p
p
p
p

cresc.

String Quintet in E-flat Major, K.614

tr
f
p

tr
p
f

tr
p
f
sf

tr
sf
p
f

tr
p
f

tr
f
p

tr
f
p

Andante.

tr
1.
2.

p
sf
p

cresc.
f
p
sf
sfp
fp
mf
tr

cresc.
f
tr
fp
p
mf
sf
sfp

f
p
mf
p
sf
p
sfp

MENUETTO.
Allegretto.

Trio.
tr
p
f
cresc.
mfp

cresc.
mfp
f
p
tr
M.D.C.
Allegro.
sf

tr
p
sf
f

f
p
sfp
tr

sf
p
p
sf
p
sf
p
sf
p
f
f
f
f
f

staccato
staccato
staccato

tr
p
f
sf
mf
mfp